Low-Carb Recipes

Favorite Brand Name™

Low-Carb Recipes

Publications International, Ltd.

Favorite Brand Name Recipes at www.fbnr.com

Pictured on the front cover: Pepper Steak *(page 20)*.

Pictured on the back cover *(top to bottom)*: Herbed Mushroom Vegetable Medley *(page 72)*, Scallop and Spinach Salad *(page 82)* and Pork Tenderlion with Sherry-Mushroom Sauce *(page 14)*.

ISBN: 1-4127-2034-6

Manufactured in China.

8 7 6 5 4 3 2 1

Nutritional Analysis: Nutritional information is given for the recipes in this publication. Each analysis is based on the food items in the ingredient list, except ingredients labeled as "optional" or "for garnish." When more than one ingredient choice is listed, the first ingredient is used for analysis. If a range for the amount of an ingredient is given, the nutritional analysis is based on the lowest amount. Foods offered as "serve with" suggestions are not included in the analysis unless otherwise stated.

Microwave Cooking: Microwave ovens vary in wattage. Use the cooking times as guidelines and check for doneness before adding more time.

Preparation/Cooking Times: Preparation times are based on the approximate amount of time required to assemble the recipe before cooking, baking, chilling or serving. These times include preparation steps such as measuring, chopping and mixing. The fact that some preparations and cooking can be done simultaneously is taken into account. Preparation of optional ingredients and serving suggestions is not included.

Low-Carb

43 RECIPES
7g carb or less!

Pleasing Beef & Pork   6

Taste-Tempting Chicken   26

Mouthwatering Seafood   46

Satisfying Salads, Sides & More   66

Index   92

Acknowledgments   94

Pleasing Beef & Pork

Rosemary Steak

4 boneless top loin beef steaks or New York strip steaks
    (about 6 ounces each)
2 tablespoons minced fresh rosemary
2 cloves garlic, minced
1 tablespoon extra-virgin olive oil
1 teaspoon grated lemon peel
1 teaspoon coarsely ground black pepper
½ teaspoon salt
    Fresh rosemary sprigs

Score steaks in diamond pattern on both sides. Combine minced rosemary, garlic, oil, lemon peel, pepper and salt in small bowl; rub mixture onto surface of meat. Cover and refrigerate at least 15 minutes. Grill steaks over medium-hot KINGSFORD® Briquets about 4 minutes per side until medium-rare or to desired doneness. Cut steaks diagonally into ½-inch-thick slices. Garnish with rosemary sprigs.   Makes 4 servings

NUTRITION INFORMATION PER SERVING

Calories	328	Fat	16
Protein	42	Sodium	392
Carbohydrate	1	Cholesterol	110

Rosemary Steak

Veal in Gingered Sweet Bell Pepper Sauce

    1 teaspoon olive oil
    ¾ pound veal cutlets, thinly sliced
    ½ cup fat-free (skim) milk
    1 tablespoon finely chopped fresh tarragon
    2 teaspoons crushed capers
    1 jar (7 ounces) roasted red peppers, drained
    1 tablespoon lemon juice
    ½ teaspoon freshly grated ginger
    ½ teaspoon black pepper

1. Heat oil in medium saucepan over high heat. Add veal; lightly brown both sides. Reduce heat to medium. Add milk, chopped tarragon and capers. Cook, uncovered, 5 minutes or until veal is fork-tender and milk evaporates.

2. Place roasted peppers, lemon juice, ginger and black pepper in food processor or blender; process until smooth. Set aside.

3. Remove veal from pan with slotted spoon; place in serving dish. Spoon roasted pepper sauce over veal. Sprinkle with cooked capers and fresh tarragon, if desired.   Makes 4 servings

NUTRITION INFORMATION PER SERVING

Calories	120	Fat	4
Protein	14	Sodium	89
Carbohydrate	6	Cholesterol	54

Veal in Gingered Sweet Bell Pepper Sauce

Grilled Beef Salad

½ cup mayonnaise

2 tablespoons cider vinegar or white wine vinegar

1 tablespoon spicy brown mustard

2 cloves garlic, minced

½ teaspoon sugar

6 cups torn assorted lettuces

1 large tomato, seeded and chopped

⅓ cup chopped fresh basil

2 slices red onion, separated into rings

1 pound boneless beef top sirloin steak, cut 1 inch thick

½ teaspoon salt

½ teaspoon black pepper

½ cup herb or garlic croutons

Prepare grill for direct cooking. Combine mayonnaise, vinegar, mustard, garlic and sugar in small bowl; mix well. Cover and refrigerate until serving.

Toss together lettuce, tomato, basil and onion in large bowl; cover and refrigerate until serving.

Sprinkle both sides of steak with salt and ½ teaspoon pepper. Place steak on grid. Grill, covered, over medium-high heat 10 minutes for medium-rare or until desired doneness is reached, turning halfway through grilling time.

Transfer steak to carving board. Slice in half lengthwise; carve crosswise into thin slices.

Add steak and croutons to bowl with lettuce mixture; toss well. Add mayonnaise mixture; toss until well coated. Serve with additional pepper, if desired.

Makes 4 servings

NUTRITION INFORMATION PER SERVING

Calories	383	Fat	30
Protein	25	Sodium	562
Carbohydrate	8	Cholesterol	75

Grilled Beef Salad

Peppercorn Beef Kabobs

    1 pound boneless beef sirloin steak, cut 1 inch thick
1½ teaspoons black peppercorns, crushed
    ½ teaspoon salt
    ½ teaspoon paprika
    1 clove garlic, minced
    1 medium onion, cut into 12 wedges
        Cherry tomato halves (optional)

Cut beef steak into 1-inch pieces. Combine peppercorns, salt, paprika and garlic in shallow dish. Add beef; toss to coat. Thread an equal number of beef pieces onto each of four 12-inch skewers along with 3 onion wedges. (If using bamboo skewers, soak in water for 20 to 30 minutes before using to prevent them from burning.) Place kabobs on rack in broiler pan. Broil 3 to 4 inches from heat source 9 to 12 minutes, turning occasionally. Garnish with tomatoes, if desired.   Makes 4 servings

NUTRITION INFORMATION PER SERVING

Calories	158	Fat	4
Protein	25	Sodium	339
Carbohydrate	3	Cholesterol	54

Peppercorn Beef Kabobs

Pork Tenderloin with Sherry-Mushroom Sauce

- 1 pork tenderloin (1 to 1½ pounds)
- 1½ cups chopped fresh mushrooms or shiitake mushroom caps
- 2 tablespoons sliced green onion
- 1 clove garlic, minced
- 1 tablespoon reduced-calorie margarine
- 1 tablespoon cornstarch
- 1 tablespoon chopped fresh parsley
- ½ teaspoon dried thyme leaves, crushed
  Dash black pepper
- ⅓ cup water
- 1 tablespoon dry sherry
- ½ teaspoon beef bouillon granules

Preheat oven to 375°F. Place pork on rack in shallow baking pan. Insert meat thermometer into thickest part of tenderloin. Roast, uncovered, 25 to 35 minutes or until thermometer registers 159°F. Let stand, covered, 5 to 10 minutes while preparing sauce.

Cook and stir mushrooms, green onion and garlic in margarine in small saucepan over medium heat until vegetables are tender. Stir in cornstarch, parsley, thyme and pepper. Stir in water, sherry and bouillon granules. Cook and stir until sauce boils and thickens. Cook and stir 2 minutes more. Slice pork; serve with sauce.

Makes 4 servings

NUTRITION INFORMATION PER SERVING

Calories	179	Fat	6
Protein	26	Sodium	205
Carbohydrate	4	Cholesterol	81

Pork Tenderloin with Sherry-Mushroom Sauce

Italian-Style Meat Loaf

    1 can (6 ounces) no-salt-added tomato paste
  ½ cup dry red wine
  ½ cup water
    1 teaspoon minced garlic
  ½ teaspoon dried basil leaves
  ½ teaspoon dried oregano leaves
  ¼ teaspoon salt
  12 ounces lean ground round
  12 ounces ground turkey breast
    1 cup fresh whole wheat bread crumbs (2 slices whole wheat
        bread)
  ½ cup shredded zucchini
  ¼ cup cholesterol-free egg substitute or 2 egg whites

1. Preheat oven to 350°F. Combine tomato paste, wine, water, garlic, basil, oregano and salt in small saucepan. Bring to a boil; reduce heat to low. Simmer, uncovered, 15 minutes. Set aside.

2. Combine beef, turkey, bread crumbs, zucchini, egg substitute and ½ cup reserved tomato mixture in large bowl. Mix well. Shape into loaf; place into ungreased 9×5×3-inch loaf pan. Bake 45 minutes. Discard any drippings. Pour ½ cup remaining tomato mixture over top of loaf. Bake an additional 15 minutes. Place on serving platter. Cool 10 minutes before slicing. Garnish as desired.   Makes 8 servings

NUTRITION INFORMATION PER SERVING

Calories	144	Fat	2
Protein	19	Sodium	171
Carbohydrate	7	Cholesterol	41

Italian-Style Meat Loaf

Joe's Special

1 pound lean ground beef
2 cups sliced mushrooms
1 small onion, chopped
2 teaspoons Worcestershire sauce
1 teaspoon dried oregano leaves
1 teaspoon ground nutmeg
½ teaspoon garlic powder
½ teaspoon salt
1 package (10 ounces) frozen chopped spinach, thawed
4 large eggs, lightly beaten
⅓ cup grated Parmesan cheese

1. Spray large skillet with nonstick cooking spray. Add ground beef, mushrooms and onion; cook over medium-high heat 6 to 8 minutes or until onion is tender, breaking beef apart with wooden spoon. Add Worcestershire, oregano, nutmeg, garlic powder and salt. Cook until meat is no longer pink.

2. Drain spinach (do not squeeze dry); stir into meat mixture. Push mixture to one side of pan. Reduce heat to medium. Pour eggs into other side of pan; cook, without stirring, 1 to 2 minutes or until set on bottom. Lift eggs to allow uncooked portion to flow underneath. Repeat until softly set. Gently stir into meat mixture and heat through. Stir in cheese.   *Makes 4 to 6 servings*

SERVING SUGGESTION: Serve with salsa.

NUTRITION INFORMATION PER SERVING

Calories	369	Fat	23
Protein	32	Sodium	614
Carbohydrate	8	Cholesterol	290

Joe's Special

Pepper Steak

1 tablespoon coarsely cracked black pepper
½ teaspoon dried rosemary
2 beef filet mignons or rib-eye steaks, 1 inch thick
   (4 to 6 ounces each)
1 tablespoon butter or margarine
1 tablespoon vegetable oil
¼ cup brandy or dry red wine

1. Combine pepper and rosemary in bowl. Coat both sides of steaks with mixture.

2. Heat butter and oil in large skillet until hot; add steaks and cook over medium to medium-high heat 5 to 7 minutes per side for medium, or to desired degree of doneness. Remove steaks from skillet. Sprinkle lightly with salt and cover to keep warm.

3. Add brandy to skillet; bring to a boil over high heat, scraping particles from bottom of skillet. Boil about 1 minute or until liquid is reduced by half. Spoon sauce over steaks.   Makes 2 servings

NOTE: For a special touch, sprinkle chopped parsley over steaks before serving.

COOK'S NOTES: Filet mignon and rib-eye steaks are two of the most tender cuts of meat. These choice cuts are the most expensive and are well-suited to quick, dry-heat cooking methods such as pan-frying, roasting, broiling and grilling.

NUTRITION INFORMATION PER SERVING

Calories	392	Fat	24
Protein	25	Sodium	117
Carbohydrate	2	Cholesterol	84

Pepper Steak

Jamaican Steak

2 pounds beef flank steak
¼ cup packed brown sugar
3 tablespoons orange juice
3 tablespoons lime juice
3 cloves garlic, minced
1 piece (1½×1 inches) fresh ginger, minced
2 teaspoons grated orange peel
2 teaspoons grated lime peel
1 teaspoon salt
1 teaspoon black pepper
¼ teaspoon ground cinnamon
⅛ teaspoon ground cloves
   Shredded orange peel
   Shredded lime peel

Score both sides of beef.* Combine sugar, juices, garlic, ginger, grated peels, salt, pepper, cinnamon and cloves in 2-quart glass dish. Add beef; turn to coat. Cover and refrigerate steak at least 2 hours. Remove beef from marinade; discard marinade. Grill beef over medium-hot KINGSFORD® Briquets about 6 minutes per side until medium-rare or to desired doneness. Garnish with shredded orange and lime peels.   Makes 6 servings

*To score flank steak, cut ¼-inch-deep diagonal lines about 1 inch apart in surface of steak to form diamond-shaped design.

NUTRITION INFORMATION PER SERVING

Calories	283	
Protein	30	
Carbohydrate	0	
Fat	17	
Sodium	97	
Cholesterol	81	

Jamaican Steak

Pork Medallions with Marsala

1 pound pork tenderloin, cut into ½-inch slices
   All-purpose flour
2 tablespoons olive oil
1 clove garlic, minced
½ cup sweet Marsala wine
2 tablespoons chopped fresh parsley

1. Lightly dust pork with flour. Heat oil in large skillet over medium-high heat until hot. Add pork slices; cook 3 minutes per side or until browned. Remove from pan. Reduce heat to medium.

2. Add garlic to skillet; cook and stir 1 minute. Add wine and pork; cook 3 minutes or until pork is barely pink in center. Remove pork from skillet. Stir in parsley. Simmer wine mixture until slightly thickened, 2 to 3 minutes.   *Makes 4 servings*

TIP: For a special touch, sprinkle with chopped red onion just before serving.

COOK'S NOTES: Marsala is rich smoky-flavored wine imported from the Mediterranean island of Sicily. This sweet varietal is served with dessert or used for cooking. Dry Marsala is served as a before-dinner drink.

NUTRITION INFORMATION PER SERVING

Calories	*218*	*Fat*	*11*
Protein	*24*	*Sodium*	*67*
Carbohydrate	*1*	*Cholesterol*	*65*

Pork Medallions with Marsala

Taste-Tempting Chicken

Grilled Rosemary Chicken

2 tablespoons lemon juice
2 tablespoons olive oil
2 cloves garlic, minced
2 tablespoons minced fresh rosemary
¼ teaspoon salt
4 boneless skinless chicken breasts

1. Whisk together lemon juice, oil, garlic, rosemary and salt in small bowl. Pour into shallow glass dish. Add chicken, turning to coat both sides with lemon juice mixture. Cover and marinate in refrigerator 15 minutes, turning chicken once.

2. Grill chicken over medium-hot coals 5 to 6 minutes per side or until chicken is no longer pink in center.   Makes 4 servings

COOK'S NOTES: For added flavor, moisten a few sprigs of fresh rosemary and toss on the hot coals just before grilling. Store rosemary in the refrigerator for up to five days. Wrap sprigs in a barely damp paper towel and place in a sealed plastic bag.

NUTRITION INFORMATION PER SERVING

Calories	156	Fat	5
Protein	25	Sodium	104
Carbohydrate	<1	Cholesterol	69

Grilled Rosemary Chicken

Japanese Yakitori

1 pound boneless skinless chicken breast halves, cut into
¾-inch-wide strips
2 tablespoons sherry or pineapple juice
2 tablespoons reduced-sodium soy sauce
1 tablespoon sugar
1 tablespoon peanut oil
½ teaspoon minced garlic
½ teaspoon minced ginger
5 ounces red pearl onions
½ fresh pineapple, cut into 1-inch wedges

1. Place chicken in large heavy-duty resealable plastic food storage bag. Combine sherry, soy sauce, sugar, oil, garlic and ginger in small bowl; mix thoroughly to dissolve sugar. Pour into plastic bag with chicken; seal bag and turn to coat thoroughly. Refrigerate 30 minutes or up to 2 hours, turning occasionally. (If using wooden or bamboo skewers, prepare by soaking skewers in water 20 to 30 minutes to keep from burning.)

2. Meanwhile, place onions in boiling water for 4 minutes; drain and cool in ice water to stop cooking. Cut off root ends and slip off outer skins; set aside.

3. Drain chicken, reserving marinade. Weave chicken accordion-style onto skewers, alternating onions and pineapple with chicken. Brush with reserved marinade; discard remaining marinade.

4. Grill on uncovered grill over medium-hot coals 6 to 8 minutes or until chicken is no longer pink in center, turning once.

Makes 6 servings

NUTRITION INFORMATION PER SERVING

Calories	124	Fat	3
Protein	17	Sodium	99
Carbohydrate	6	Cholesterol	46

Japanese Yakitori

Lemon Pepper Chicken

⅓ cup lemon juice
¼ cup finely chopped onion
¼ cup olive oil
1 tablespoon brown sugar
1 tablespoon cracked black pepper
3 cloves garlic, minced
2 teaspoons grated lemon peel
¾ teaspoon salt
4 chicken quarters (about 2½ pounds)

Combine lemon juice, onion, oil, sugar, pepper, garlic, lemon peel and salt in small bowl; reserve 2 tablespoons marinade. Combine remaining marinade and chicken in large resealable plastic food storage bag. Seal bag; knead to coat. Refrigerate at least 4 hours or overnight.

Remove chicken from marinade; discard marinade. Arrange chicken on microwavable plate; cover with waxed paper. Microwave at HIGH 5 minutes. Turn and rearrange chicken. Cover and microwave at HIGH 5 minutes.

Transfer chicken to grill. Grill covered over medium-hot coals 15 to 20 minutes or until juices run clear, turning several times and basting often with reserved marinade.   Makes 4 servings

NUTRITION INFORMATION PER SERVING

Calories 375	Fat. 23
Protein. 37	Sodium 256
Carbohydrate 3	Cholesterol 129

Lemon Pepper Chicken

Chicken Roll-Ups

¼ cup fresh lemon juice
1 tablespoon olive oil
¼ teaspoon salt
¼ teaspoon black pepper
4 boneless skinless chicken breast halves
¼ cup finely chopped fresh Italian parsley
2 tablespoons grated Parmesan cheese
2 tablespoons chopped fresh chives
1 teaspoon finely grated lemon peel
2 large cloves garlic, pressed in garlic press
16 toothpicks soaked in hot water 15 minutes

1. Combine lemon juice, oil, salt and pepper in 11×7-inch casserole. Pound chicken to ⅜-inch thickness. Place chicken in lemon mixture; turn to coat. Cover; marinate in refrigerator at least 30 minutes.

2. Prepare grill for direct cooking.

3. Combine parsley, cheese, chives, lemon peel and garlic in small bowl. Discard chicken marinade. Spread ¼ of parsley mixture over each chicken breast, leaving an inch around edges free. Starting at narrow end, roll chicken to enclose filling; secure with toothpicks.

4. Grill chicken, covered, over medium-hot coals about 2 mintues on each side or until golden brown. Transfer chicken to low or indirect heat; grill, covered, about 5 minutes or until chicken is no longer pink in center. Remove toothpicks; slice chicken breast.

Makes 4 servings

NUTRITION INFORMATION PER SERVING

Calories	159	Fat	5
Protein	27	Sodium	155
Carbohydrate	1	Cholesterol	71

Chicken Roll-Up

Chicken Broccoli Frittata

1 cup chopped fresh broccoli flowerettes
½ cup chopped cooked chicken
¼ cup chopped tomato
¼ cup chopped onion
¼ teaspoon dried tarragon leaves
1 tablespoon FLEISCHMANN'S® Original Margarine
1 cup EGG BEATERS® Healthy Real Egg Product

In 10-inch nonstick skillet, over medium heat, sauté broccoli, chicken, tomato, onion and tarragon in margarine until broccoli is tender-crisp. Reduce heat to low. Pour Egg Beaters® evenly into skillet over chicken mixture. Cover; cook for 5 to 7 minutes or until cooked on bottom and almost set on top. Slide onto serving platter; cut into wedges to serve. *Makes 2 servings*

NUTRITION INFORMATION PER SERVING

Calories	187	Fat	7
Protein	24	Sodium	308
Carbohydrate	7	Cholesterol	27

Chicken Teriyaki

8 large chicken drumsticks (about 2 pounds)
⅓ cup teriyaki sauce
2 tablespoons brandy or apple juice
1 green onion, minced
1 tablespoon vegetable oil
1 teaspoon ground ginger
½ teaspoon sugar
¼ teaspoon garlic powder
Prepared sweet and sour sauce (optional)

Remove skin from drumsticks, if desired, by pulling skin toward end of leg with paper towel; discard skin.

Place chicken in large resealable plastic food storage bag. Combine teriyaki sauce, brandy, onion, oil, ginger, sugar and garlic powder in small bowl; pour over chicken. Close bag securely, turning to coat. Marinate in refrigerator at least 1 hour or overnight, turning occasionally.

Prepare grill for indirect cooking.

Drain chicken; reserve marinade. Place chicken on grid directly over drip pan. Grill, covered, over medium-high heat 60 minutes or until chicken is no longer pink in center and juices run clear, turning and brushing with reserved marinade every 20 minutes. Discard remaining marinade. Serve with sweet and sour sauce, if desired.

Makes 4 servings

NUTRITION INFORMATION PER SERVING

Calories	224	Fat	8
Protein	26	Sodium	1003
Carbohydrate	5	Cholesterol	82

Chicken Scaloppine with Lemon-Caper Sauce

1 pound boneless skinless chicken breasts
3 tablespoons all-purpose flour, divided
¼ teaspoon black pepper
¼ teaspoon chili powder
½ cup fat-free, reduced-sodium chicken broth
1 tablespoon lemon juice
1 tablespoon drained capers
½ teaspoon olive oil

1. Place chicken breasts, one at a time, between sheets of waxed paper. Pound to ¼-inch thickness. Combine 2 tablespoons flour, pepper and chili powder in shallow plate. Dip chicken pieces in flour mixture to lightly coat both sides.

2. Combine broth, lemon juice, remaining flour and capers in small bowl.

3. Spray large skillet with nonstick cooking spray; heat over medium-high heat. Place chicken in hot pan in single layer; cook 1½ minutes. Turn over; cook 1 to 1½ minutes or until chicken is no longer pink in center. Repeat with remaining chicken (brush pan with ¼ teaspoon oil each time you add pieces to prevent sticking). If cooking more than 2 batches, reduce heat to medium to prevent burning chicken.

4. Stir broth mixture and pour into skillet. Boil 1 to 2 minutes or until thickened. Serve immediately over chicken.   Makes 4 servings

NUTRITION INFORMATION PER SERVING

Calories	144	Fat	4
Protein	22	Sodium	67
Carbohydrate	4	Cholesterol	58

Chicken Scaloppine with Lemon-Caper Sauce

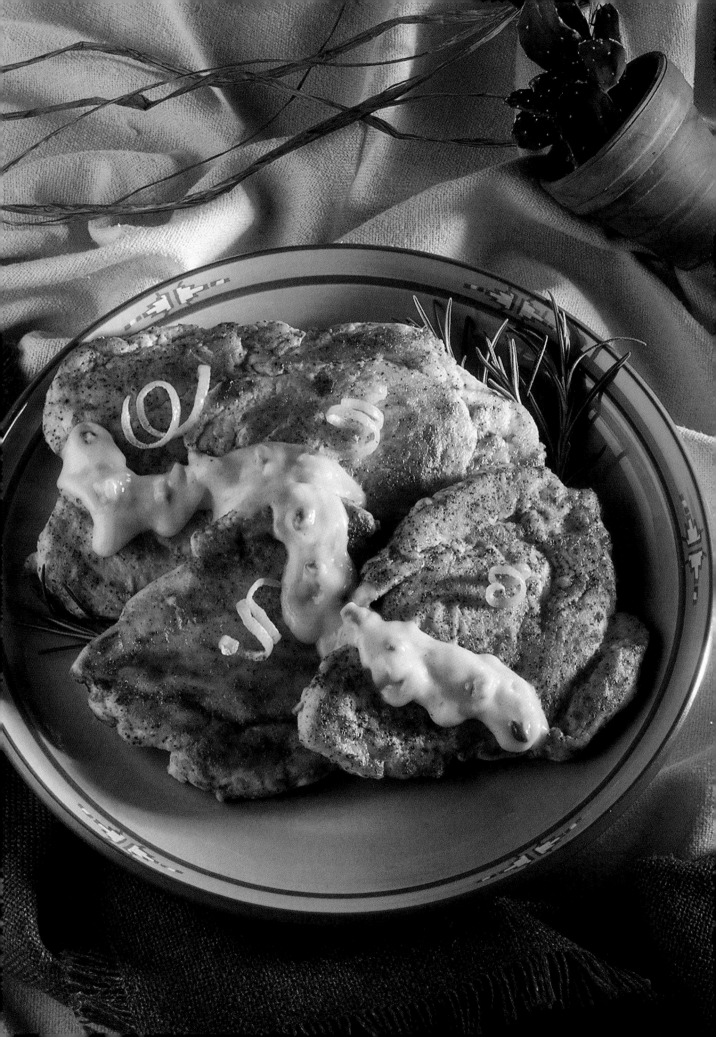

Balsamic Chicken

6 boneless skinless chicken breast halves
1½ teaspoons fresh rosemary leaves, minced *or* ½ teaspoon
    dried rosemary
2 cloves garlic, minced
¾ teaspoon black pepper
½ teaspoon salt
1 tablespoon olive oil
¼ cup good-quality balsamic vinegar

1. Rinse chicken and pat dry. Combine rosemary, garlic, pepper and salt in small bowl; mix well. Place chicken in large bowl; drizzle chicken with oil and rub with spice mixture. Cover and refrigerate overnight.

2. Preheat oven to 450°F. Spray heavy roasting pan or iron skillet with nonstick cooking spray. Place chicken in pan; bake 10 minutes. Turn chicken over, stirring in 3 to 4 tablespoons water if drippings begin to stick to pan.

3. Bake about 10 minutes or until chicken is golden brown and no longer pink in center. If pan is dry, stir in another 1 to 2 tablespoons water to loosen drippings.

4. Drizzle balsamic vinegar over chicken in pan. Transfer chicken to plates. Stir liquid in pan; drizzle over chicken. Garnish, if desired.

Makes 6 servings

NUTRITION INFORMATION PER SERVING

Calories 174	Fat 5
Protein 27	Sodium 242
Carbohydrate 3	Cholesterol 73

Balsamic Chicken

Oriental Chicken Kabobs

1 pound boneless skinless chicken breasts
2 small zucchini or yellow squash, cut into 1-inch slices
8 large fresh mushrooms
1 cup red, yellow or green bell pepper pieces
2 tablespoons reduced-sodium soy sauce
2 tablespoons dry sherry
1 teaspoon dark sesame oil
2 cloves garlic, minced
2 large green onions, cut into 1-inch pieces

1. Cut chicken into 1½-inch pieces; place in large plastic bag. Add zucchini, mushrooms and bell pepper to bag. Combine soy sauce, sherry, oil and garlic in cup; pour over chicken and vegetables. Close bag securely; turn to coat. Marinate in refrigerator at least 30 minutes or up to 4 hours.

2. Soak 4 (12-inch) skewers in water to cover 20 minutes.

3. Drain chicken and vegetables; reserve marinade. Alternately thread chicken and vegetables with onions onto skewers.

4. Place on rack of broiler pan. Brush with half of reserved marinade. Broil 5 to 6 inches from heat 5 minutes. Turn kabobs over; brush with remaining marinade. Broil 5 minutes or until chicken is no longer pink. Garnish with green onion brushes, if desired.

Makes 4 servings

NUTRITION INFORMATION PER SERVING

Calories	135	Fat	3
Protein	19	Sodium	307
Carbohydrate	6	Cholesterol	46

Oriental Chicken Kabobs

Persian Chicken Breasts

1 medium lemon
2 teaspoons olive oil
1 teaspoon ground cinnamon
½ teaspoon salt
¼ teaspoon black pepper
¼ teaspoon turmeric
4 boneless skinless chicken breast halves

1. Peel lemon rind into long strips with paring knife; reserve for garnish, if desired. Juice lemon; combine juice with oil, cinnamon, salt, pepper and turmeric in large heavy-duty resealable plastic food storage bag. Gently knead bag to mix ingredients thoroughly; add chicken. Seal bag and turn to coat thoroughly. Refrigerate 4 hours or overnight.

2. Remove chicken from marinade and gently shake to remove excess. Grill chicken 5 to 7 minutes per side or until chicken is no longer pink in center, brushing occasionally with marinade. Discard remaining marinade. Serve chicken with grilled vegetables, if desired.

Makes 4 servings

NUTRITION INFORMATION PER SERVING

Calories	143	Fat	4
Protein	25	Sodium	149
Carbohydrate	1	Cholesterol	69

Blue Cheese Stuffed Chicken Breasts

2 tablespoons margarine or butter, softened, divided
½ cup (2 ounces) crumbled blue cheese
¾ teaspoon dried thyme leaves
2 whole boneless chicken breasts with skin (not split)
1 tablespoon bottled or fresh lemon juice
½ teaspoon paprika

1. Prepare grill for grilling. Combine 1 tablespoon margarine, blue cheese and thyme in small bowl until blended. Season with salt and pepper.

2. Loosen skin over breast of chicken by pushing fingers between skin and meat, taking care not to tear skin. Spread blue cheese mixture under skin with a rubber spatula or small spoon; massage skin to evenly spread cheese mixture.

3. Place chicken, skin side down, on grid over medium coals. Grill over covered grill 5 minutes. Meanwhile, melt remaining 1 tablespoon margarine; stir in lemon juice and paprika. Turn chicken; brush with lemon juice mixture. Grill 5 to 7 minutes more or until chicken is no longer pink in center. Transfer chicken to carving board; cut each breast in half.   *Makes 4 servings*

SERVING SUGGESTION: Serve with steamed broccoli.

NUTRITION INFORMATION PER SERVING

Calories	296	Fat	17
Protein	32	Sodium	333
Carbohydrate	1	Cholesterol	93

Chicken Marsala

4 BUTTERBALL® Boneless Skinless Chicken Breast Fillets
3 cups sliced fresh mushrooms
2 tablespoons sliced green onion
2 tablespoons water
¼ teaspoon salt
¼ cup dry Marsala wine
1 teaspoon cornstarch

Flatten chicken fillets between two pieces of plastic wrap. Spray nonstick skillet with nonstick cooking spray; heat over medium heat until hot. Add chicken; cook 2 to 3 minutes on each side or until no longer pink in center. Transfer to platter; keep warm. Add mushrooms, onion, water and salt to skillet. Cook 3 minutes or until most of the liquid has evaporated. Combine wine and cornstarch in small bowl; add to skillet. Heat, stirring constantly, until thickened. Spoon over warm chicken.   Makes 4 servings

NUTRITION INFORMATION PER SERVING

Calories	161	Fat	3
Protein	26	Sodium	209
Carbohydrate	3	Cholesterol	69

Chicken Marsala

Mouthwatering Seafood

Red Snapper Vera Cruz

    4 red snapper fillets (1 pound)
¼ cup fresh lime juice
    1 tablespoon fresh lemon juice
    1 teaspoon chili powder
    4 green onions with 4 inches of tops, sliced in ½-inch lengths
    1 tomato, coarsely chopped
½ cup chopped Anaheim or green bell pepper
½ cup chopped red bell pepper

1. Place red snapper in shallow round microwavable baking dish. Combine lime juice, lemon juice and chili powder. Pour over snapper. Marinate 10 minutes, turning once or twice.

2. Sprinkle green onions, tomato and peppers over snapper. Cover dish loosely with vented plastic wrap. Microwave at HIGH 6 minutes or just until snapper flakes in center, rotating dish every 2 minutes. Let stand, covered, 4 minutes.   Makes 4 servings

NUTRITION INFORMATION PER SERVING

Calories	144	Fat	2
Protein	24	Sodium	61
Carbohydrate	7	Cholesterol	42

Red Snapper Vera Cruz

Beijing Fillet of Sole

        2 tablespoons reduced-sodium soy sauce
        2 teaspoons dark sesame oil
        4 sole fillets (6 ounces each)
    1¼ cups preshredded cabbage or coleslaw mix
      ½ cup crushed chow mein noodles
        1 egg white, slightly beaten
        2 teaspoons sesame seeds
        1 package (10 ounces) frozen snow peas, cooked and
            drained

1. Heat oven to 350°F. Combine soy sauce and oil in small bowl. Place sole in shallow dish. Lightly brush both sides of sole with soy mixture.

2. Combine cabbage, crushed noodles, egg white and remaining soy mixture in small bowl. Spoon evenly over sole. Roll up each fillet and place, seam side down, in shallow foil-lined roasting pan.

3. Sprinkle rolls with sesame seeds. Bake 25 to 30 minutes until fish flakes when tested with fork. Serve with snow peas.

Makes 4 servings

NUTRITION INFORMATION PER SERVING

Calories.............................252		Fat.................................8
Protein...............................34		Sodium.............................435
Carbohydrate..........................6		Cholesterol.........................80

Beijing Fillet of Sole

Grilled Five-Spice Fish with Garlic Spinach

1½ teaspoons finely shredded lime peel
3 tablespoons fresh lime juice
4 teaspoons minced fresh ginger
½ to 1 teaspoon Chinese 5-spice powder
½ teaspoon sugar
½ teaspoon salt
⅛ teaspoon black pepper
2 teaspoons vegetable oil, divided
1 pound salmon steaks
½ pound fresh baby spinach leaves (about 8 cups lightly packed), washed
2 large cloves garlic, pressed through garlic press

1. Combine lime peel, lime juice, ginger, 5-spice powder, sugar, salt, pepper and 1 teaspoon oil in 2-quart dish. Add salmon; turn to coat. Cover; refrigerate 2 to 3 hours.

2. Combine spinach, garlic and remaining 1 teaspoon oil in 3-quart microwaveable dish; toss. Cover; microwave on HIGH (100% power) 2 minutes or until spinach is wilted. Drain; keep warm. Meanwhile, prepare barbecue grill for direct cooking.

3. Remove salmon from marinade and place on oiled grid. Brush salmon with portion of marinade. Grill salmon, covered, over medium-hot coals 4 minutes. Turn salmon; brush with marinade and grill 4 minutes or until salmon flakes easily with fork. Discard marinade. Serve fish over bed of spinach.   *Makes 4 servings*

NUTRITION INFORMATION PER SERVING

Calories	169	Fat	6
Protein	24	Sodium	409
Carbohydrate	5	Cholesterol	57

Grilled Five-Spice Fish with Garlic Spinach

Dilled Salmon in Parchment

2 skinless salmon fillets (4 to 6 ounces each)
2 tablespoons butter or margarine, melted
1 tablespoon lemon juice
1 tablespoon chopped fresh dill
1 tablespoon chopped shallots

1. Preheat oven to 400°F. Cut 2 pieces parchment paper into 12-inch squares; fold squares in half diagonally and cut into half heart shapes. Open parchment; place fish fillet on one side of each heart.

2. Combine butter and lemon juice in small cup; drizzle over fish. Sprinkle with dill, shallots and salt and pepper to taste.

3. Fold parchment hearts in half. Beginning at top of heart, fold edges together, 2 inches at a time. At tip of heart, fold parchment over to seal.

4. Bake fish about 10 minutes or until parchment pouch puffs up. To serve, cut an "X" through top layer of parchment and fold back points to display contents.   Makes 2 servings

NUTRITION INFORMATION PER SERVING

Calories	234	Fat	15
Protein	22	Sodium	191
Carbohydrate	2	Cholesterol	88

Dilled Salmon in Parchment

Crispy Oven Fried Fish Fingers

½ cup seasoned dry bread crumbs
1 tablespoon grated Parmesan cheese
2 teaspoons grated lemon peel
¾ teaspoon dried marjoram leaves
½ teaspoon paprika
¼ teaspoon dried thyme leaves
⅛ teaspoon garlic powder
4 cod fillets (about 1 pound)
3 tablespoons lemon juice
2 tablespoons dry white wine or water
1 tablespoon CRISCO® Vegetable Oil

1. Heat oven to 425°F. Oil 13×9×2-inch pan lightly.

2. Combine bread crumbs, Parmesan cheese, lemon peel, marjoram, paprika, thyme and garlic powder in shallow dish.

3. Rinse fish fillets. Pat dry.

4. Combine lemon juice and wine in separate shallow dish. Cut fish into desired size "fingers" or "sticks." Dip each fish finger into lemon mixture, then into crumb mixture, coating well. Place in pan. Drizzle with oil.

5. Bake at 425°F for 10 to 12 minutes or until fish flakes easily with fork. Let stand 2 to 3 minutes in pan. Remove to serving plate. Garnish, if desired.

Makes 4 servings

NUTRITION INFORMATION PER SERVING (¼ OF RECIPE)

Calories	175	Fat	6
Protein	24	Sodium	180
Carbohydrate	7	Cholesterol	60

Crispy Oven Fried Fish Fingers

Garlic Skewered Shrimp

1 pound large shrimp, peeled and deveined
2 tablespoons reduced-sodium soy sauce
1 tablespoon vegetable oil
3 cloves garlic, minced
¼ teaspoon red pepper flakes (optional)
3 green onions, cut into 1-inch pieces

Prepare grill or preheat broiler. Soak 4 bamboo (12-inch) skewers in water 20 minutes. Meanwhile, place shrimp in large plastic bag. Combine soy sauce, oil, garlic and red pepper in cup; mix well. Pour over shrimp. Close bag securely; turn to coat. Marinate at room temperature 15 minutes.

Drain shrimp; reserve marinade. Alternately thread shrimp and onions onto skewers. Place skewers on grid or rack of broiler pan. Brush with reserved marinade; discard any remaining marinade. Grill, covered, over medium-hot coals or broil 5 to 6 inches from heat 5 minutes on each side or until shrimp are pink and opaque. Serve on lettuce-lined plate.   Makes 4 servings

TIP: For a more attractive presentation, leave the tails on the shrimp.

NUTRITION INFORMATION PER SERVING

Calories 102	Fat 2
Protein 19	Sodium 287
Carbohydrate . . . . <1	Cholesterol 174

Garlic Skewered Shrimp

Broiled Hunan Fish Fillets

3 tablespoons reduced-sodium soy sauce
1 tablespoon finely chopped green onion
2 teaspoons dark sesame oil
1 clove garlic, minced
1 teaspoon minced fresh ginger
¼ teaspoon red pepper flakes
   Nonstick cooking spray
1 pound red snapper, scrod or cod fillets

1. Combine soy sauce, onion, oil, garlic, ginger and red pepper flakes in small bowl.

2. Spray rack of broiler pan with nonstick cooking spray. Place fish on rack; brush with soy sauce mixture.

3. Broil 4 to 5 inches from heat 10 minutes or until fish flakes easily with fork. Serve on lettuce-lined plate, if desired.

Makes 4 servings

NUTRITION INFORMATION PER SERVING

Calories	144	Fat	4
Protein	25	Sodium	446
Carbohydrate	1	Cholesterol	42

Broiled Hunan Fish Fillets

Trout Stuffed with Fresh Mint and Oranges

 2 pan-dressed* trout (1 to 1¼ pounds each)
½ teaspoon coarse salt, such as Kosher salt
 1 orange, sliced
 1 cup fresh mint leaves
 1 sweet onion, sliced

*A pan-dressed trout has been gutted and scaled with head and tail removed.

1. Rinse trout under cold running water; pat dry with paper towels.

2. Sprinkle cavities of trout with salt; fill each with orange slices and mint. Cover each fish with onion slices.

3. Spray 2 large sheets of foil with nonstick cooking spray. Place 1 fish on each sheet and seal using Drugstore Wrap technique.**

4. Place foil packets seam-side down directly on medium-hot coals; grill on covered grill 20 to 25 minutes or until trout flakes easily when tested with fork, turning once.

5. Carefully open foil packets; remove and discard orange-mint stuffing and trout skin. Serve immediately.   Makes 6 servings

**Place food in the center of an oblong piece of heavy-duty foil, leaving at least a two-inch border around the food. Bring the two long sides together above the food; fold down in a series of locked folds, allowing for heat circulation and expansion. Fold short ends up and over again. Press folds firmly to seal the foil packet.

NUTRITION INFORMATION PER SERVING

Calories	203	Fat	5
Protein	32	Sodium	220
Carbohydrate	5	Cholesterol	87

Grilled Swordfish à l'Orange

4 swordfish, halibut or shark steaks (about 1½ pounds)
1 orange
¾ cup orange juice
1 tablespoon lemon juice
1 tablespoon sesame oil
1 tablespoon soy sauce
1 teaspoon cornstarch
   Salt and black pepper to taste

Rinse swordfish and pat dry with paper towels. Grate enough orange peel to measure 1 teaspoon; set aside. Peel orange and pull apart into sections; set aside. Combine orange juice, lemon juice, oil and soy sauce in small bowl. Pour half of orange juice mixture into shallow glass dish. Add ½ teaspoon grated orange peel to orange juice mixture. Place fish in dish; turn to coat in mixture. Cover and allow to marinate in refrigerator at least 1 hour.

Place remaining half of orange juice mixture in small saucepan. Stir in cornstarch and remaining ½ teaspoon orange peel. Heat over medium-high heat, stirring constantly, 3 to 5 minutes or until sauce thickens; set aside.

Remove fish from marinade; discard remaining marinade. Lightly sprinkle fish with salt and pepper. Grill over medium coals 3 to 4 minutes per side or until fish is opaque and flakes easily when tested with fork. Top with reserved orange sections and orange sauce. Serve immediately.   Makes 4 servings

NUTRITION INFORMATION PER SERVING

Calories	243	Fat	8
Protein	34	Sodium	772
Carbohydrate	7	Cholesterol	67

Pineapple Salsa Topped Halibut

Pineapple Salsa

- ¾ cup diced fresh pineapple *or* 1 can (8 ounces) unsweetened pineapple tidbits, drained
- 2 tablespoons finely chopped red bell pepper
- 2 tablespoons chopped cilantro
- 2 teaspoons vegetable oil
- 1 teaspoon bottled minced ginger or finely shredded fresh ginger
- 1 teaspoon bottled minced jalapeño pepper or fresh jalapeño pepper

Halibut

- 4 halibut or swordfish steaks (6 ounces each), cut about ¾-inch thick
- 1 tablespoon garlic-flavored olive oil*
- ¼ teaspoon salt

*Or, add ¼ teaspoon bottled minced garlic to 1 tablespoon olive oil.

1. For salsa, combine pineapple, bell pepper, cilantro, oil, ginger and jalapeño pepper in small bowl; mix well. Cover; refrigerate up to 2 days.

2. Prepare barbecue grill for direct cooking. Brush halibut with oil; sprinkle with salt.

3. Grill halibut, on uncovered grill, over medium-hot coals 8 minutes or until halibut flakes easily when tested with fork, turning once.

4. Top halibut with salsa; serve immediately.   Makes 4 servings

NUTRITION INFORMATION PER SERVING

Calories	253	Fat	10
Protein	36	Sodium	237
Carbohydrate	4	Cholesterol	55

Pineapple Salsa Topped Halibut

Maryland Crab Cakes

1 pound fresh backfin crabmeat, cartilage removed
10 low-salt crackers (2 inches each), crushed to equal ½ cup
    crumbs
1 rib celery, finely chopped
1 green onion, finely chopped
¼ cup cholesterol-free egg substitute
3 tablespoons nonfat tartar sauce
1 teaspoon seafood seasoning
2 teaspoons vegetable oil

1. Combine crabmeat, cracker crumbs, celery and onion in medium bowl; set aside.

2. Mix egg substitute, tartar sauce and seafood seasoning in small bowl; pour over crabmeat mixture. Gently mix so large lumps will not be broken. Shape into six ¾-inch-thick patties. Cover; refrigerate 30 minutes.

3. Spray skillet with nonstick cooking spray. Add oil; heat over medium-high heat. Place crab cakes in skillet; cook 3 to 4 minutes each side or until cakes are lightly browned. Garnish with lemon wedges, if desired.   *Makes 6 servings*

NUTRITION INFORMATION PER SERVING

Calories	127	Fat	4
Protein	14	Sodium	382
Carbohydrate	8	Cholesterol	44

Maryland Crab Cakes

Satisfying Salads, Sides & More

BLT Chicken Salad for Two

2 boneless skinless chicken breast halves
¼ cup mayonnaise or salad dressing
½ teaspoon black pepper
4 large leaf lettuce leaves
1 large tomato, seeded and diced
3 slices crisp-cooked bacon, crumbled
1 hard-cooked egg, sliced
   Additional mayonnaise or salad dressing

1. Brush chicken with mayonnaise; sprinkle with pepper. Grill over hot coals 5 to 7 minutes per side or until no longer pink in center. Cool slightly; cut into thin strips.

2. Arrange lettuce leaves on serving plates. Top with chicken, tomato, bacon and egg. Spoon additional mayonnaise over top.

Makes 2 servings

NUTRITION INFORMATION PER SERVING

Calories	444	Fat	34
Protein	32	Sodium	390
Carbohydrate	4	Cholesterol	194

BLT Chicken Salad for Two

Ratatouille

½ pound eggplant, cut into ½-inch cubes
1 small onion, sliced and separated into rings
1 small zucchini, thinly sliced
½ medium green bell pepper, chopped
1 tomato, cut into wedges
1 tablespoon grated Parmesan cheese
1 rib celery, chopped
¼ teaspoon salt (optional)
¼ teaspoon dried chervil leaves
¼ teaspoon dried oregano leaves
⅛ teaspoon instant minced garlic
⅛ teaspoon dried thyme leaves
Dash ground pepper

Microwave Directions
Combine all ingredients in 2-quart microwavable casserole; cover. Microwave at HIGH 7 to 10 minutes or until eggplant is translucent, stirring every 3 minutes.   *Makes 6 servings*

NUTRITION INFORMATION PER SERVING

Calories	29	Fat	1
Protein	1	Sodium	29
Carbohydrate	6	Cholesterol	1

Ratatouille

Hot and Spicy Spinach

Nonstick cooking spray
1 red bell pepper, cut into 1-inch pieces
1 clove garlic, minced
1 pound prewashed fresh spinach, rinsed and chopped
1 tablespoon prepared mustard
1 teaspoon lemon juice
¼ teaspoon red pepper flakes

1. Spray large skillet with nonstick cooking spray; heat over medium heat. Add red bell pepper and garlic; cook and stir 3 minutes.

2. Add spinach; cook and stir 3 minutes or just until spinach begins to wilt.

3. Stir in mustard, lemon juice and red pepper flakes. Serve immediately.

Makes 4 servings

COOK'S TIP: To obtain the maximum nutritional value from spinach, cook it for the shortest possible time. The vitamins in spinach and other greens are soluble in water and fats and are therefore lost during long cooking.

NUTRITION INFORMATION PER SERVING

Calories 37	Fat 1
Protein 4	Sodium 138
Carbohydrate 6	Cholesterol 0

Hot and Spicy Spinach

Herbed Mushroom Vegetable Medley

4 ounces button or crimini mushrooms

1 medium red or yellow bell pepper, cut into ¼-inch-wide strips

1 medium zucchini, cut crosswise into ¼-inch-thick slices

1 medium yellow squash, cut crosswise into ¼-inch-thick slices

3 tablespoons butter or margarine, melted

1 tablespoon chopped fresh thyme leaves *or* 1 teaspoon dried thyme leaves, crushed

1 tablespoon chopped fresh basil leaves *or* 1 teaspoon dried basil leaves, crushed

1 tablespoon chopped fresh chives or green onion tops

1 clove garlic, minced

¼ teaspoon salt

¼ teaspoon black pepper

1. Prepare barbecue grill for direct cooking.

2. Cut thin slice from base of mushroom stems with paring knife; discard. Thinly slice mushroom stems and caps. Combine mushrooms, bell pepper, zucchini and squash in large bowl. Combine remaining ingredients in small bowl. Pour over vegetable mixture; toss to coat well.

3. Transfer mixture to 20×14-inch sheet of heavy-duty foil; wrap. Place foil packet on grid. Grill packet, on covered grill, over medium coals 20 to 25 minutes or until vegetables are fork-tender. Open packet carefully to serve.   *Makes 4 to 6 servings*

NUTRITION INFORMATION PER SERVING

Calories	34	Fat	2
Protein	1	Sodium	119
Carbohydrate	3	Cholesterol	0

Herbed Mushroom Vegetable Medley

Italian Broccoli with Tomatoes

4 cups broccoli florets
½ cup water
½ teaspoon dried Italian seasoning
½ teaspoon dried parsley flakes
¼ teaspoon salt (optional)
⅛ teaspoon black pepper
2 medium tomatoes, cut into wedges
½ cup shredded part-skim mozzarella cheese

Microwave Directions

Place broccoli and water in 2-quart microwavable casserole; cover. Microwave at HIGH (100% power) 5 to 8 minutes or until crisp-tender. Drain. Stir in Italian seasoning, parsley, salt, pepper and tomatoes. Microwave, uncovered, at HIGH (100% power) 2 to 4 minutes or until tomatoes are hot. Sprinkle with cheese. Microwave 1 minute or until cheese melts.   Makes 6 servings

NUTRITION INFORMATION PER SERVING

Calories	50	Fat	2
Protein	4	Sodium	64
Carbohydrate	5	Cholesterol	5

Italian Broccoli with Tomatoes

Grilled Turkey Ham Quesadillas

    Nonstick cooking spray
¼ cup salsa
 4 (7-inch) flour tortillas
½ cup shredded reduced-sodium reduced-fat Monterey Jack
    cheese
¼ cup finely chopped turkey ham
 1 can (4 ounces) diced green chilies, drained
    Additional salsa (optional)
    Nonfat sour cream (optional)

1. To prevent sticking, spray grid with cooking spray. Prepare coals for grilling.

2. Spread 1 tablespoon salsa on each tortilla. Sprinkle cheese, turkey ham and chilies equally over half of each tortilla; fold over uncovered half to make "sandwich"; spray tops and bottoms of tortilla "sandwiches" with cooking spray.

3. Grill quesadillas on uncovered grill over medium coals 1½ minutes per side or until cheese is melted and tortillas are golden brown, turning once. Quarter each quesadilla and serve with additional salsa and nonfat sour cream, if desired.

Makes 8 servings

NUTRITION INFORMATION PER SERVING

Calories	66	Fat	2
Protein	4	Sodium	195
Carbohydrate	8	Cholesterol	5

Sunset Fruit Salad

2 cups boiling water
1 package (4-serving size) JELL-O® Brand Cranberry Flavor
 Sugar Free Low Calorie Gelatin Dessert or JELL-O® Brand
 Cranberry Flavor Gelatin Dessert, or any red flavor
½ cup cold water
1 can (8 ounces) sliced peaches in juice, drained, chopped
1 package (4-serving size) JELL-O® Brand Orange Flavor
 Sugar Free Low Calorie Gelatin Dessert or JELL-O® Brand
 Orange Flavor Gelatin Dessert
1 can (8 ounces) crushed pineapple in juice, undrained

STIR 1 cup of the boiling water into cranberry gelatin in medium bowl at least 2 minutes until completely dissolved. Stir in cold water. Refrigerate about 45 minutes or until slightly thickened (consistency of unbeaten egg whites). Stir in peaches. Spoon into 5-cup mold. Refrigerate about 15 minutes or until set but not firm (gelatin should stick to finger when touched and should mound).

MEANWHILE, stir remaining 1 cup boiling water into orange gelatin in medium bowl at least 2 minutes until completely dissolved. Stir in pineapple with juice. Pour over gelatin layer in mold.

REFRIGERATE 4 hours or until firm. Unmold. Garnish as desired.   Makes 10 servings

NUTRITION INFORMATION PER SERVING (USING JELL-O® BRAND CRANBERRY AND ORANGE FLAVORS SUGAR FREE LOW CALORIE GELATIN DESSERT AND OMITTING GARNISH):

Calories	30	Fat	0
Protein	1	Sodium	60
Carbohydrate	6	Cholesterol	0

Roman Spinach Soup

6 cups ⅓-less-salt chicken broth

1 cup cholesterol-free egg substitute

¼ cup minced fresh basil

3 tablespoons freshly grated Parmesan cheese

2 tablespoons lemon juice

1 tablespoon minced fresh parsley

¼ teaspoon white pepper

⅛ teaspoon ground nutmeg

8 cups fresh spinach, washed, stems removed, chopped

1. Bring broth to a boil in 4-quart saucepan over medium heat.

2. Beat together egg substitute, basil, Parmesan cheese, lemon juice, parsley, white pepper and nutmeg in small bowl. Set aside.

3. Stir spinach into broth; simmer 1 minute. Slowly pour egg mixture into broth mixture, whisking constantly so egg threads form. Simmer 2 to 3 minutes or until egg is cooked. Garnish with lemon slices, if desired. Serve immediately.

Makes 8 (¾-cup) servings

NOTE: Soup may look curdled.

NUTRITION INFORMATION PER SERVING

Calories	46	Fat	1
Protein	6	Sodium	153
Carbohydrate	4	Cholesterol	2

Roman Spinach Soup

Frenched Beans with Celery

¾ **pound fresh green beans**
2 **ribs celery**
¼ **cup water**
2 **tablespoons butter, melted**
2 **tablespoons toasted sunflower seeds***
  Celery leaves and carrot slices for garnish

*To toast sunflower seeds, heat ½ teaspoon oil in small skillet over medium heat. Add shelled sunflower seeds; cook and stir 3 minutes or until lightly browned, shaking pan constantly. Remove with slotted spoon to paper towels.

1. Place beans in colander; rinse well. To prepare beans, snap off stem end from each bean, pulling strings down to remove if present. (Young tender beans may have no strings.)

2. Slice beans lengthwise; set aside.

3. To prepare celery, trim stem end and leaves from ribs. Reserve leaves for garnish, if desired. Slice ribs thin on the diagonal.

4. Bring 1 inch of water in 2-quart saucepan to a boil over high heat. Add beans and celery. Cover; reduce heat to medium-low. Simmer 8 minutes or until beans are crisp-tender; drain.

5. Toss beans and celery with butter. Transfer to warm serving dish. Sprinkle with sunflower seeds. Garnish, if desired. Serve immediately.   Makes 6 side-dish servings

NUTRITION INFORMATION PER SERVING

Calories	70	Fat	6
Protein	2	Sodium	62
Carbohydrate	4	Cholesterol	0

Frenched Beans wtih Celery

Scallop and Spinach Salad

1 package (10 ounces) spinach leaves, washed, stemmed
    and torn
3 thin slices red onion, halved and separated
12 ounces sea scallops
    Ground red pepper
    Paprika
    Nonstick cooking spray
½ cup prepared fat-free Italian salad dressing
¼ cup crumbled blue cheese
2 tablespoons toasted walnuts

1. Pat spinach dry; place in large bowl with red onion. Cover; set aside.

2. Rinse scallops. Cut in half horizontally (to make 2 thin rounds); pat dry. Sprinkle top side lightly with red pepper and paprika. Spray large nonstick skillet with cooking spray; heat over high heat until very hot. Add half of scallops, seasoned side down, in single layer, placing ½ inch or more apart. Sprinkle with red pepper and paprika. Cook 2 minutes or until browned on bottom. Turn scallops; cook 1 to 2 minutes or until opaque in center. Transfer to plate; cover to keep warm. Wipe skillet clean; repeat procedure with remaining scallops.

3. Place dressing in small saucepan; bring to a boil over high heat. Pour dressing over spinach and onion; toss to coat. Divide among 4 plates. Place scallops on top of spinach; sprinkle with blue cheese and walnuts. *Makes 4 servings*

NUTRITION INFORMATION PER SERVING

Calories	169	Fat	6
Protein	24	Sodium	660
Carbohydrate	6	Cholesterol	50

Scallop and Spinach Salad

Stir-Fry Beef & Vegetable Soup

1 pound boneless beef steak, such as sirloin or round steak
2 teaspoons dark sesame oil, divided
3 cans (about 14 ounces each) reduced-sodium beef broth
1 package (16 ounces) frozen stir-fry vegetables
3 green onions, thinly sliced
¼ cup stir-fry sauce

1. Slice beef across grain into ⅛-inch-thick strips; cut strips into bite-size pieces.

2. Heat Dutch oven over high heat. Add 1 teaspoon oil and tilt pan to coat bottom. Add half the beef in single layer; cook 1 minute, without stirring, until slightly browned on bottom. Turn and brown other side about 1 minute. Remove beef from pan with slotted spoon; set aside. Repeat with remaining 1 teaspoon oil and beef; set aside.

3. Add broth to Dutch oven; cover and bring to a boil over high heat. Add vegetables; reduce heat to medium-high and simmer 3 to 5 minutes or until heated through. Add beef, green onions and stir-fry sauce; simmer 1 minute more.   Makes 6 servings

NUTRITION INFORMATION PER SERVING

Calories 159	Fat 5
Protein 20	Sodium 356
Carbohydrate 7	Cholesterol 43

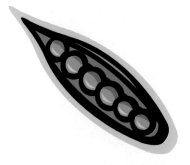

Marinated Mushrooms, Carrots and Snow Peas

1 cup julienne carrots
1 cup fresh snow peas or sugar snap peas
½ cup water
1 lemon
2 cups small mushrooms
⅔ cup white wine vinegar
2 tablespoons sugar
2 tablespoons extra-light olive oil
1 clove garlic, minced
2 tablespoons chopped fresh parsley
1 tablespoon chopped fresh thyme

1. Combine carrots and peas in 1-quart microwavable dish; add ½ cup water. Cover and microwave at HIGH 4 minutes or just until water boils. Do not drain.

2. Remove several strips of peel from lemon with vegetable peeler. Chop peel to measure 1 teaspoon. Squeeze juice from lemon to measure 2 tablespoons. Combine peel, juice and remaining ingredients in small bowl. Pour over carrot mixture. Cover and refrigerate at least 3 hours.

3. To serve, remove vegetables from marinade with slotted spoon. Place in serving dish; discard marinade.

Makes 12 servings

NUTRITION INFORMATION PER SERVING

Calories	30	Fat	1
Protein	1	Sodium	5
Carbohydrate	4	Cholesterol	0

Crab Cobb Salad

12 cups washed and torn romaine lettuce

2 cans (6 ounces each) crabmeat, drained

2 cups diced ripe tomatoes or halved cherry tomatoes

¼ cup (1½ ounces) crumbled blue or Gorgonzola cheese

¼ cup cholesterol-free bacon bits

¾ cup fat-free Italian or Caesar salad dressing

Black pepper

1. Arrange lettuce on large serving platter. Arrange crabmeat, tomatoes, blue cheese and bacon bits in rows attractively over lettuce.

2. Just before serving, drizzle dressing evenly over salad; toss well. Transfer to 8 chilled serving plates; sprinkle with pepper to taste.

Makes 8 servings

NUTRITION INFORMATION PER SERVING

Calories	110	Fat	3
Protein	12	Sodium	666
Carbohydrate	8	Cholesterol	46

Crab Cobb Salad

Easy Greek Salad

6 leaves romaine lettuce, torn into 1½-inch pieces
1 cucumber, peeled and sliced
1 tomato, chopped
½ cup sliced red onion
1 ounce feta cheese, crumbled (about ⅓ cup)
2 tablespoons extra-virgin olive oil
2 tablespoons lemon juice
1 teaspoon dried oregano leaves
½ teaspoon salt

1. Combine lettuce, cucumber, tomato, onion and cheese in large serving bowl.

2. Whisk together oil, lemon juice, oregano and salt in small bowl. Pour over lettuce mixture; toss until coated. Serve immediately.

Makes 6 servings

SERVING SUGGESTION: This simple but delicious salad makes a great accompaniment for grilled steaks or chicken.

NUTRITION INFORMATION PER SERVING

Calories	72	Fat	6
Protein	2	Sodium	234
Carbohydrate	5	Cholesterol	4

Easy Greek Salad

Light Lemon Cauliflower

¼ cup chopped fresh parsley, divided
½ teaspoon grated lemon peel
6 cups (about 1½ pounds) cauliflower florets
1 tablespoon reduced-fat margarine
3 cloves garlic, minced
2 tablespoons fresh lemon juice
¼ cup grated Parmesan cheese

1. Place 1 tablespoon parsley, lemon peel and about 1 inch of water in large saucepan. Place cauliflower in steamer basket and place in saucepan. Bring water to a boil over medium heat. Cover and steam 14 to 16 minutes or until cauliflower is crisp-tender. Remove to large bowl; keep warm. Reserve ½ cup hot liquid.

2. Heat margarine in small saucepan over medium heat. Add garlic; cook and stir 2 to 3 minutes or until soft. Stir in lemon juice and reserved liquid.

3. Spoon lemon sauce over cauliflower. Sprinkle with remaining 3 tablespoons parsley and cheese before serving. Garnish with lemon slices, if desired.

Makes 6 servings

NUTRITION INFORMATION PER SERVING

Calories 53
Protein 4
Carbohydrate 6

Fat 2
Sodium 116
Cholesterol 3

Light Lemon Cauliflower

Index

Balsamic Chicken, 38
Beef (*see also* **Beef, Ground**)
   Jamaican Steak, 22
   Pepper Steak, 20
   Peppercorn Beef Kabobs, 12
   Rosemary Steak, 6
Beef, Ground
   Italian-Style Meat Loaf, 16
   Joe's Special, 18
Beijing Fillet of Sole, 48
Bell Peppers
   Herbed Mushroom Vegetable
     Medley, 72
   Hot and Spicy Spinach, 70
   Oriental Chicken Kabobs, 40
   Ratatouille, 68
   Red Snapper Vera Cruz, 46
   Veal in Gingered Sweet Bell
     Pepper Sauce, 8
BLT Chicken Salad for Two, 66
Blue Cheese Stuffed Chicken
   Breasts, 43
Broccoli
   Chicken Broccoli Frittata, 34
   Italian Broccoli with Tomatoes,
     74
Broiled Hunan Fish Fillets, 58

Chicken (*see also pages 26–44*)
   BLT Chicken Salad for Two, 66
Chicken Broccoli Frittata, 34
Chicken Marsala, 44
Chicken Roll-Ups, 32
Chicken Scaloppine with Lemon-
    Caper Sauce, 36
Chicken Teriyaki, 35
Crab
   Crab Cobb Salad, 86
   Maryland Crab Cakes, 64
Crispy Oven Fried Fish Fingers, 54

Dilled Salmon in Parchment, 52

Easy Greek Salad, 88
Egg Dishes
   Chicken Broccoli Frittata, 34
   Joe's Special, 18

Fish (*see also* **Salmon**)
   Beijing Fillet of Sole, 48
   Broiled Hunan Fish Fillets, 58
   Crispy Oven Fried Fish Fingers,
     54
   Grilled Swordfish a L'Orange, 61
   Pineapple Salsa Topped Halibut,
     62
   Red Snapper Vera Cruz, 46
   Trout Stuffed with Fresh Mint
     and Oranges, 60
Frenched Beans with Celery, 80

Garlic Skewered Shrimp, 56
Grilled Beef Salad, 10
Grilled Five-Spice Fish with Garlic
    Spinach, 50
Grilled Rosemary Chicken, 26
Grilled Swordfish a L'Orange, 61
Grilled Turkey Ham Quesadillas,
   76

Herbed Mushroom Vegetable
    Medley, 72
Hot and Spicy Spinach, 70

Italian Broccoli with Tomatoes,
   74
Italian-Style Meat Loaf, 16

Jamaican Steak, 22
Japanese Yakitori, 28
Joe's Special, 18

Lemon Pepper Chicken, 30
Light Lemon Cauliflower, 90

Marinated Mushrooms, Carrots and
 Snow Peas, 85
Maryland Crab Cakes, 64
Mushrooms
 Chicken Marsala, 44
 Herbed Mushroom Vegetable
  Medley, 72
 Joe's Special, 18
 Marinated Mushrooms, Carrots
  and Snow Peas, 85
 Pork Tenderloin with Sherry-
  Mushroom Sauce, 14

Oriental Chicken Kabobs, 40

Pepper Steak, 20
Peppercorn Beef Kabobs, 12
Persian Chicken Breasts, 42
Pineapple Salsa Topped Halibut,
 62
Pork
 BLT Chicken Salad for Two, 66
 Pork Medallions with Marsala,
  24
 Pork Tenderloin with Sherry-
  Mushroom Sauce, 14

Ratatouille, 68
Red Snapper Vera Cruz, 46
Roman Spinach Soup, 78
Rosemary Steak, 6

Salads
 BLT Chicken Salad for Two, 66
 Crab Cobb Salad, 86
 Easy Greek Salad, 88
 Grilled Beef Salad, 10
 Scallop and Spinach Salad, 82
 Sunset Fruit Salad, 77
Salmon
 Dilled Salmon in Parchment, 52
 Grilled Five-Spice Fish with
  Garlic Spinach, 50

Scallop and Spinach Salad, 82
Shellfish (*see also* **Crab**)
 Garlic Skewered Shrimp, 56
 Scallop and Spinach Salad, 82
Side Dishes
 Frenched Beans with Celery,
  80
 Herbed Mushroom Vegetable
  Medley, 72
 Hot and Spicy Spinach, 70
 Italian Broccoli with Tomatoes,
  74
 Light Lemon Cauliflower, 90
 Marinated Mushrooms, Carrots
  and Snow Peas, 85
Soup
 Roman Spinach Soup, 78
 Stir-Fry Beef & Vegetable Soup,
  84
Spinach
 Grilled Five-Spice Fish with
  Garlic Spinach, 50
 Hot and Spicy Spinach, 70
 Joe's Special, 18
 Roman Spinach Soup, 78
 Scallop and Spinach Salad, 82
Stir-Fry Beef & Vegetable Soup,
  84
Sunset Fruit Salad, 77

Trout Stuffed with Fresh Mint and
 Oranges, 60
Turkey
 Grilled Turkey Ham Quesadillas,
  76
 Italian-Style Meat Loaf, 16

Veal in Gingered Sweet Bell
 Pepper Sauce, 10

Zucchini
 Herbed Mushroom Vegetable
  Medley, 72
 Italian-Style Meat Loaf, 16
 Oriental Chicken Kabobs, 40
 Ratatouille, 68

Acknowledgments

The publisher would like to thank the companies and organizations listed below for the use of their recipes and photographs in this publication.

Butterball® Turkey Company

Egg Beaters®

The Kingsford Products Company

Kraft Foods, Inc.

The Procter & Gamble Company

METRIC CONVERSION CHART

VOLUME MEASUREMENTS (dry)

$\frac{1}{8}$ teaspoon = 0.5 mL
$\frac{1}{4}$ teaspoon = 1 mL
$\frac{1}{2}$ teaspoon = 2 mL
$\frac{3}{4}$ teaspoon = 4 mL
1 teaspoon = 5 mL
1 tablespoon = 15 mL
2 tablespoons = 30 mL
$\frac{1}{4}$ cup = 60 mL
$\frac{1}{3}$ cup = 75 mL
$\frac{1}{2}$ cup = 125 mL
$\frac{2}{3}$ cup = 150 mL
$\frac{3}{4}$ cup = 175 mL
1 cup = 250 mL
2 cups = 1 pint = 500 mL
3 cups = 750 mL
4 cups = 1 quart = 1 L

VOLUME MEASUREMENTS (fluid)

1 fluid ounce (2 tablespoons) = 30 mL
4 fluid ounces ($\frac{1}{2}$ cup) = 125 mL
8 fluid ounces (1 cup) = 250 mL
12 fluid ounces (1$\frac{1}{2}$ cups) = 375 mL
16 fluid ounces (2 cups) = 500 mL

WEIGHTS (mass)

$\frac{1}{2}$ ounce = 15 g
1 ounce = 30 g
3 ounces = 90 g
4 ounces = 120 g
8 ounces = 225 g
10 ounces = 285 g
12 ounces = 360 g
16 ounces = 1 pound = 450 g

DIMENSIONS

$\frac{1}{16}$ inch = 2 mm
$\frac{1}{8}$ inch = 3 mm
$\frac{1}{4}$ inch = 6 mm
$\frac{1}{2}$ inch = 1.5 cm
$\frac{3}{4}$ inch = 2 cm
1 inch = 2.5 cm

OVEN TEMPERATURES

250°F = 120°C
275°F = 140°C
300°F = 150°C
325°F = 160°C
350°F = 180°C
375°F = 190°C
400°F = 200°C
425°F = 220°C
450°F = 230°C

BAKING PAN SIZES

Utensil	Size in Inches/Quarts	Metric Volume	Size in Centimeters
Baking or Cake Pan (square or rectangular)	8×8×2	2 L	20×20×5
	9×9×2	2.5 L	23×23×5
	12×8×2	3 L	30×20×5
	13×9×2	3.5 L	33×23×5
Loaf Pan	8×4×3	1.5 L	20×10×7
	9×5×3	2 L	23×13×7
Round Layer Cake Pan	8×1½	1.2 L	20×4
	9×1½	1.5 L	23×4
Pie Plate	8×1¼	750 mL	20×3
	9×1¼	1 L	23×3
Baking Dish or Casserole	1 quart	1 L	—
	1½ quart	1.5 L	—
	2 quart	2 L	—